Perpetual Motion Etudes

for Piano

By Jeremy Siskind

Edited by Spencer Myer

Cover Design by Jennifer Boyd
Music Engraving by Kimberly Brand

ISBN 978-0-578-56070-0

© 2019 Jeremy Siskind

All rights reserved. International copyright secured.

No part of this book may be reproduced, stored in a retrieval system, or transmitted, in any form or by any means, (electronic, mechanical, photocopying, recording, or otherwise) without prior written permission of the author (Jeremy Siskind).

Visit Jeremy Siskind online at
www.jeremysiskind.com

From the Editor

In the *Perpetual Motion Etudes* of Jeremy Siskind, one finds a unique blend of harmonic colors, emotional journeys, and great technical demands. Through the use of a great variety of techniques, from polyrhythms to rapid hand-crossings, Siskind has created a set of pianistic paintings in which the pianist can become totally absorbed, in both the learning and performance processes. His ear for atmosphere makes for what will be an essential and standard set of studies for pianists, both classical and jazz, for years to come.

Spencer Myer

From the Composer

I've designed these etudes to be easy to read for both classical and jazz pianists. If you're a classical player, feel free to play the etudes as miniatures, skipping over the "Optional Improvisation Instructions" that follow each piece. The whole set will be short – about 20 minutes – with no improv. If you're a jazz player or interested in improvising, of course you're welcome to use whatever form, structure, or chord progression you like. However, I've provided "Instructions" for each etude to reflect the improvisation structures that have worked best for me. When I improvise, the set takes about an hour.

I highly recommend that you visit my website, www.jeremysiskind.com, for resources that will help you understand these pieces. You'll find links to versions of the scores with my personal fingerings and hand division choices; introductory videos for each etude that include practicing and improvising tips; and performance videos of me playing each piece at the Yamaha Artist Salon in New York City.

I would be thrilled if you'd stay in touch with me to share your experiences practicing and performing these pieces. I'm so glad you've chosen to add them to your repertoire!

Happy practicing,

Jeremy Siskind

Sometimes I Wander
for Nancy Woo

Jeremy Siskind

4

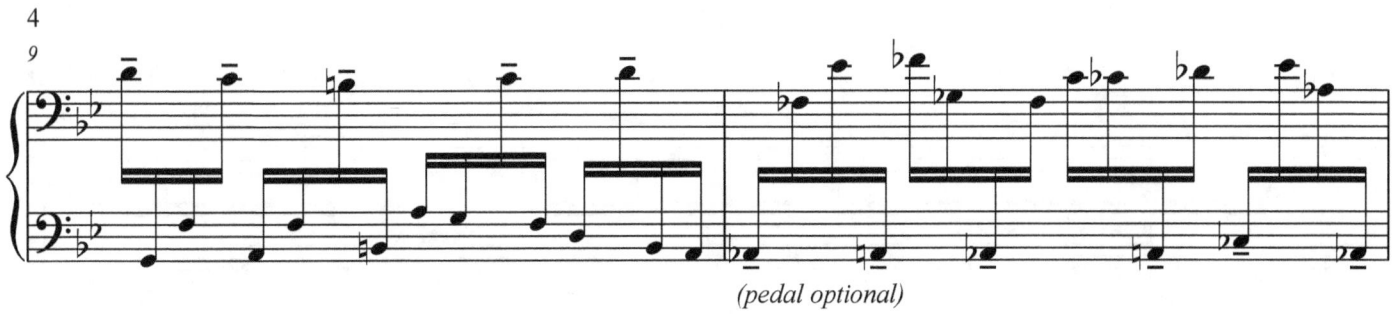

(pedal optional)

growing

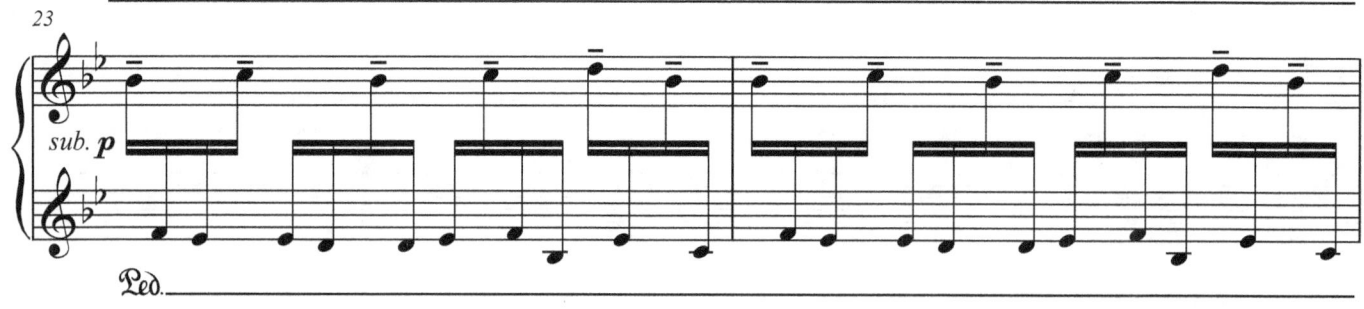
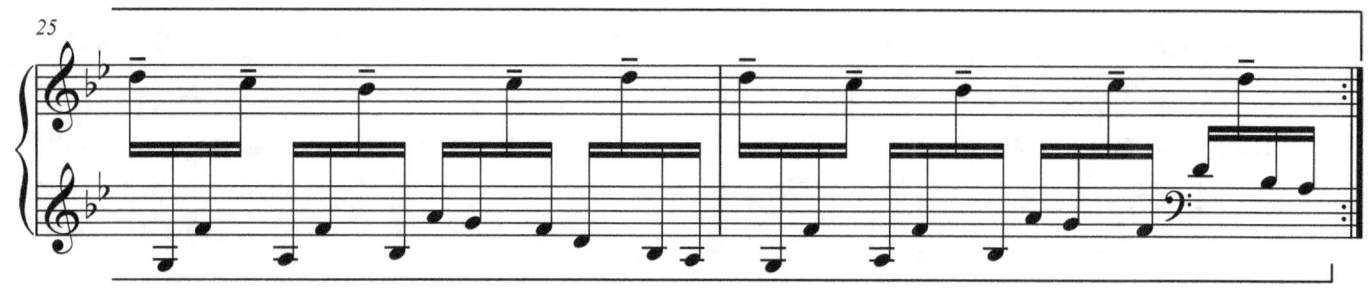

Sometimes I Wander
Optional Improvisation Instructions

Improvisation begins following measure 35. For chord changes, alternate between Gsus7 and Fsus7 for 2 measures each, occasionally inserting the figure from measure 1 as a brief "interruption."

Following the solo, repeat the written material starting from measure 28, using the figure at measure 27 as a "fanfare" to set up the through-composed music. This time, go on to take the D.S. at the end of the form and follow the directions to the coda.

Before Improvisation

Begin Improvisation

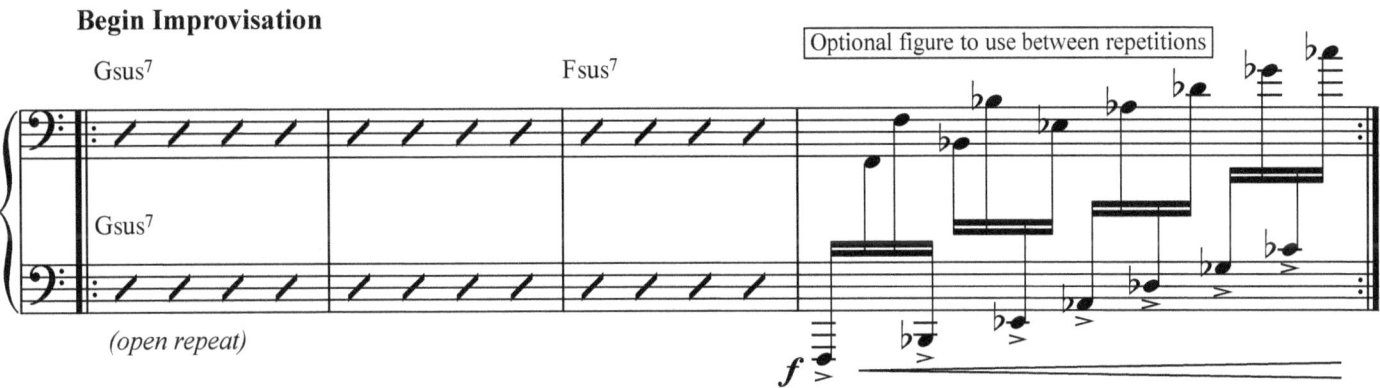

After Improvisation

last time

Return to the written material at measure 27 with the "fanfare" leading into the B section.

Try to maintain the feeling of 3-3-3-3-2-2 as a basis for your accompaniment.

One way to start the improvisation

Possible accompaniment for a right-hand improvisation

Another possible accompaniment for a right-hand improvisation

Van Gogh's Dream
for Sarah Siskind

Jeremy Siskind

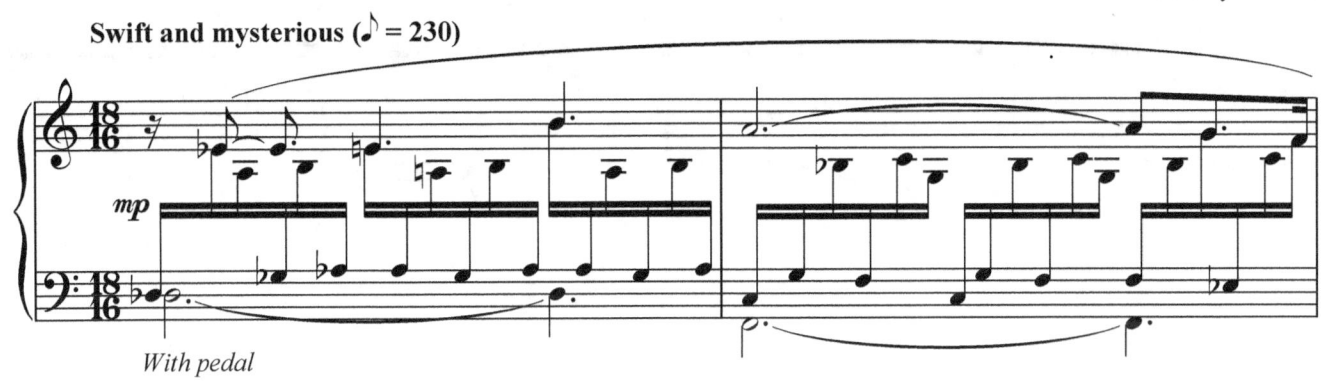

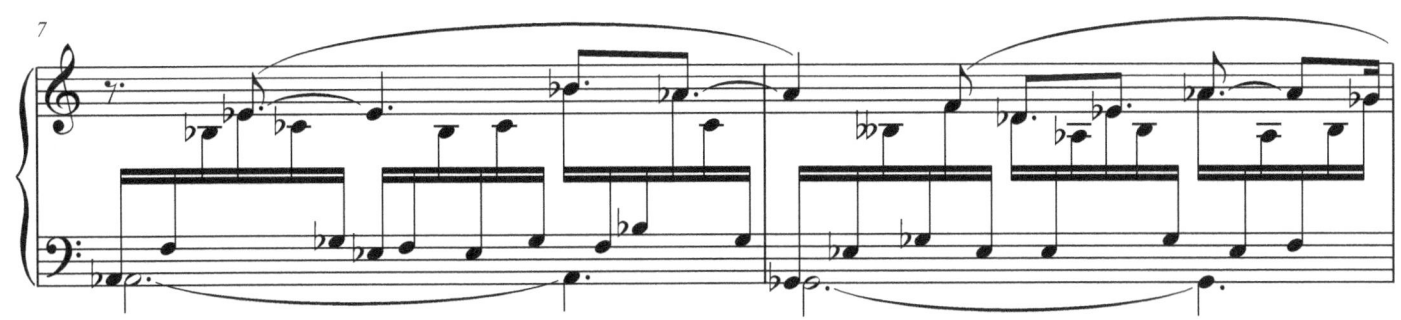

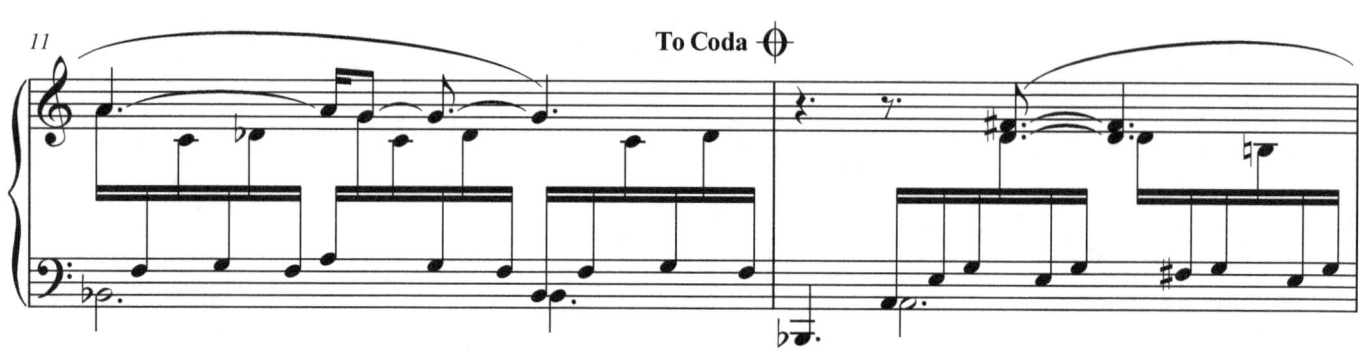
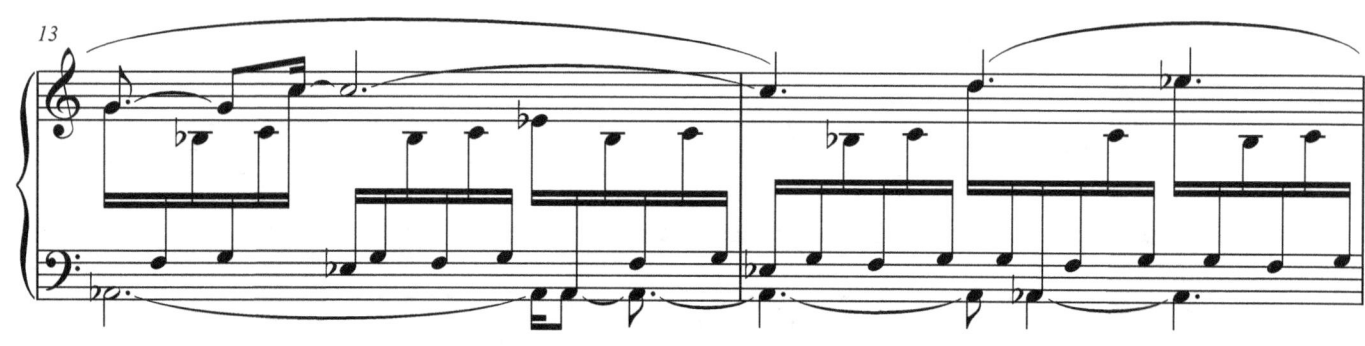
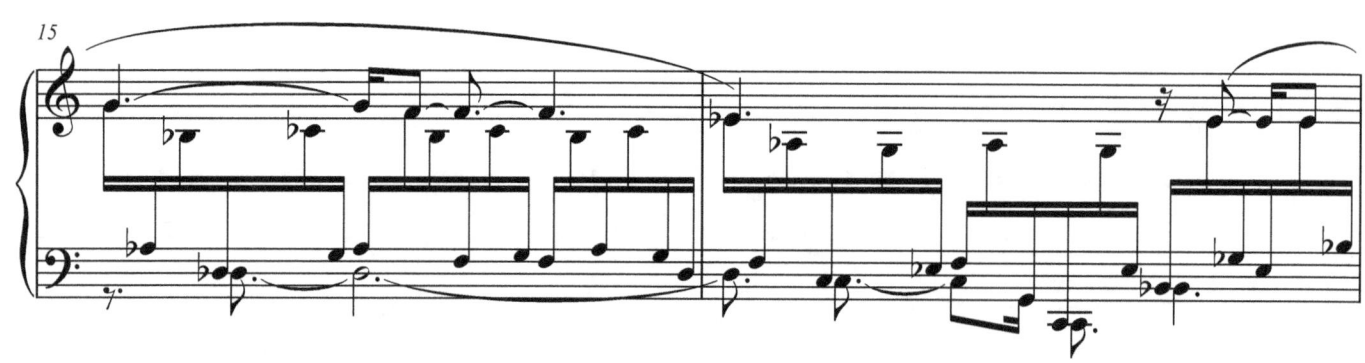

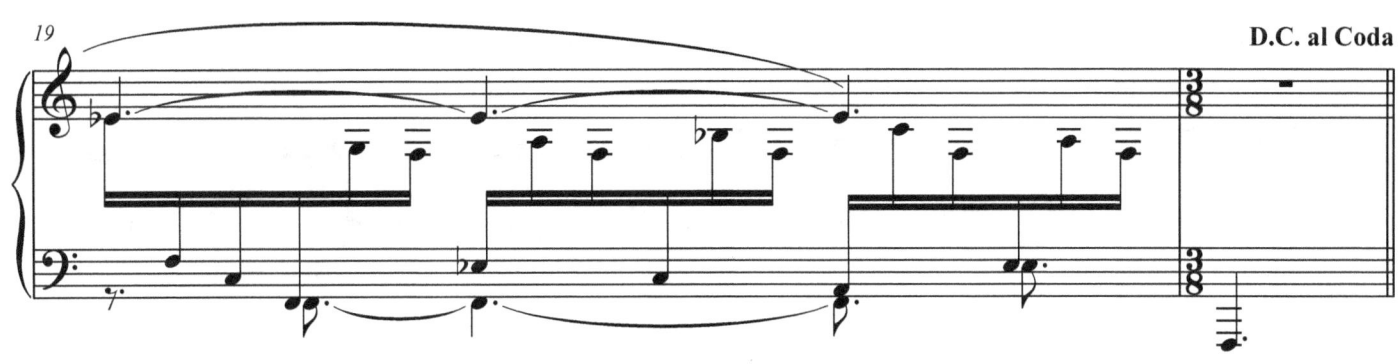

D.C. al Coda

CODA

dying away

rit.

Van Gogh's Dream
Optional Improvisation Instructions

Begin the improvisation after playing through measure 30. One possible chord progression and accompaniment texture is provided below. The accompaniment given is a suggestion for a jumping-off point, but the improviser is encouraged to change and develop the pianistic texture throughout the improvisation.

Before Improvisation

dying away   *(note slight change)*

Begin Improvisation

D.S. for more improvisation

After the last time, use this four-chord vamp to help "wind down" back into the melody.

Open repeat, dying away

After the vamp, re-enter at measure 1. Skip the 1st ending, take the 2nd ending, and finish the piece.

After Improvisation

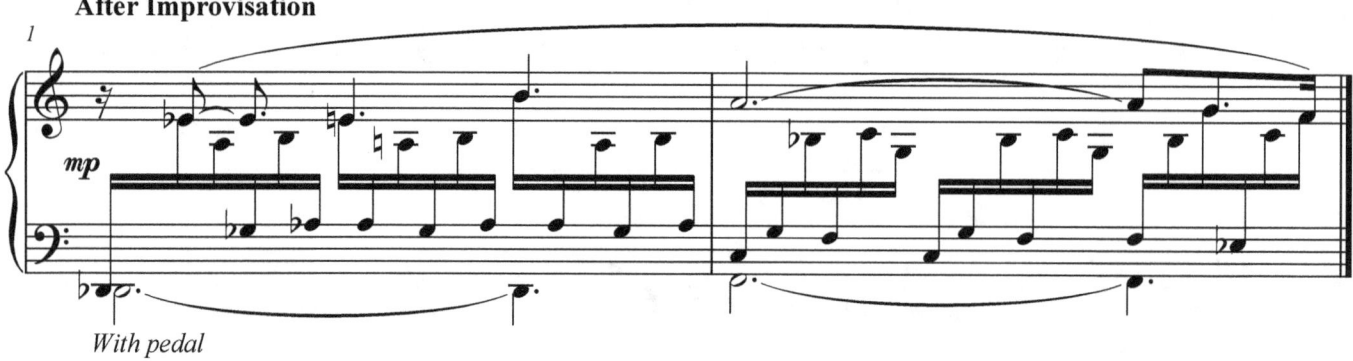

With pedal

Brooklyn Sunset

for Steve and Connie Lyman

Jeremy Siskind

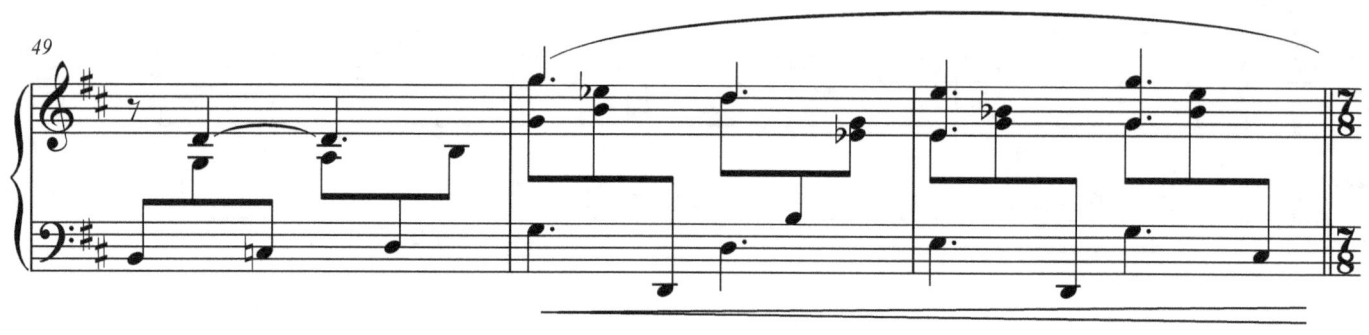

Brooklyn Sunset
Optional Improvisation Instructions

End the written section with a fermata and re-enter with a sweet and sparse texture for improvisation in 7/8.

Before Improvisation

Improvise over this 8-measure vamp consisting of "pop" chords with a descending chromatic bassline in two key centers - D and B♭.

Begin Improvisation

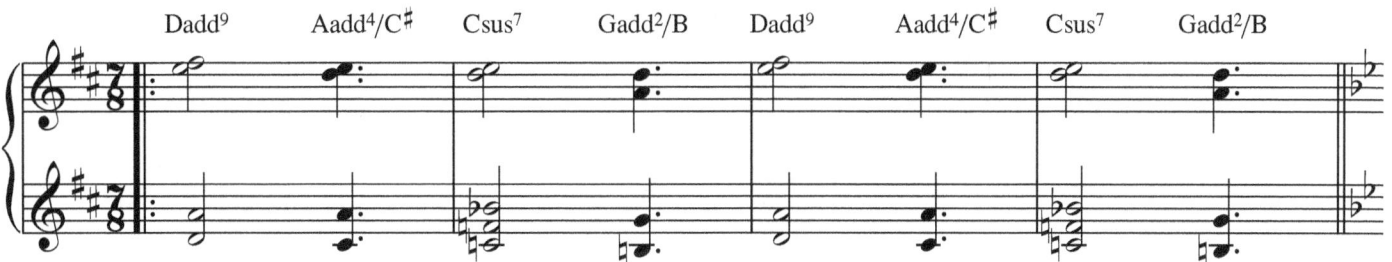

sample beginning to the improvisation, open repeat

Use this alternate progression as desired, to serve as an interlude leading back to the 8-measure vamp or leading into the through-composed section. This section could be repeated after every two times through the vamp, for instance.

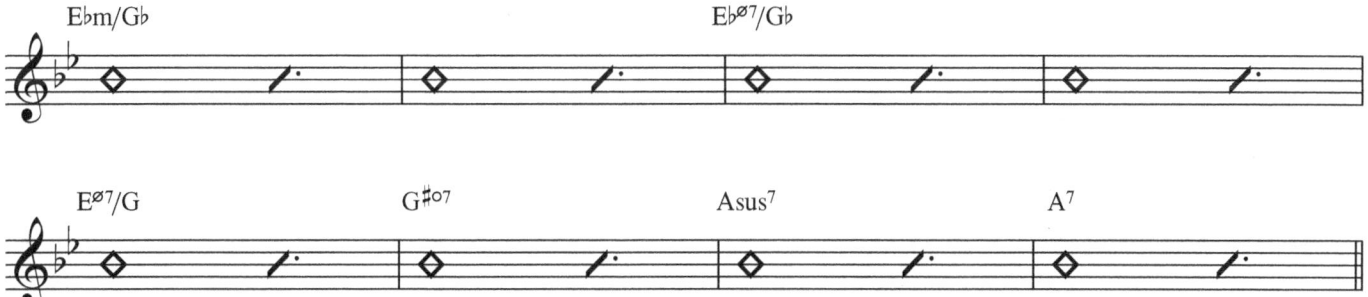

When improvisation is complete, reenter the piece at measure 52.

After Improvisation

You can also improvise on the last few chords as an ending vamp outro.
Instead of proceeding to measure 88, use the following progression as a basis for improvisation.

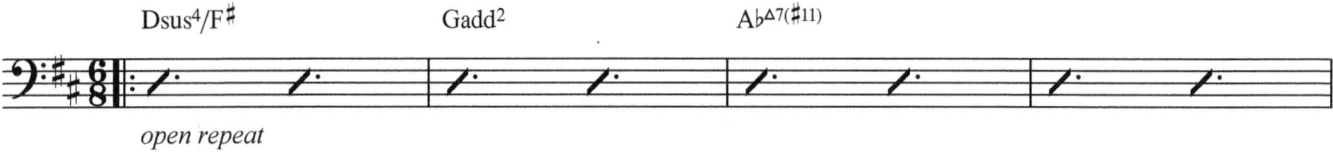

open repeat

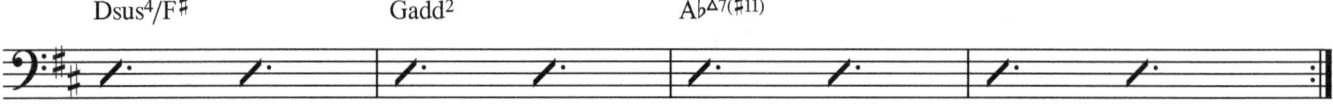

After the improvisation, reenter the piece at measure 80 and play to the end.

Homesick

Jeremy Siskind

Homesick
Optional Improvisation Instructions

> Before improvising, play the entire piece, excluding the very last measure.
> Then improvise over 15-measure form provided below in ballad style with flowing 8th notes.

Before Improvisation

Begin Improvisation

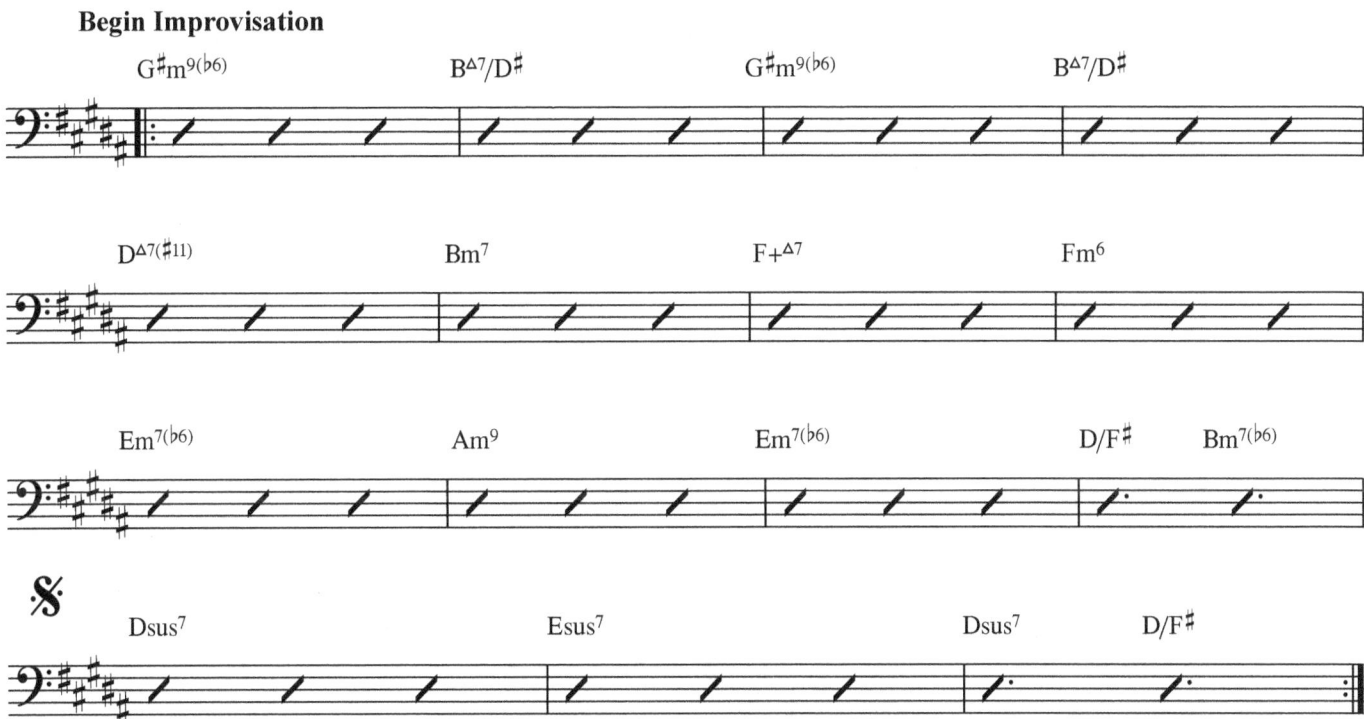

When you arrive at the "sign" for the last time, repeat a two-chord vamp of Dsus7 and Esus7 (like measures 13-14 of the written material), with the goal of slowly morphing from improvisation back into the written material, provided below.

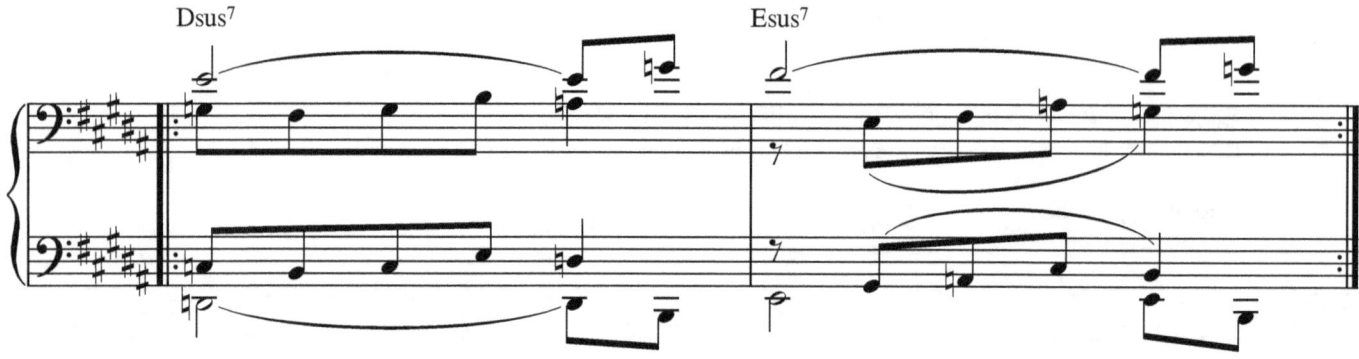

Once you've returned to the written material, continue on to measure 15 and finish the piece.

After Improvisation

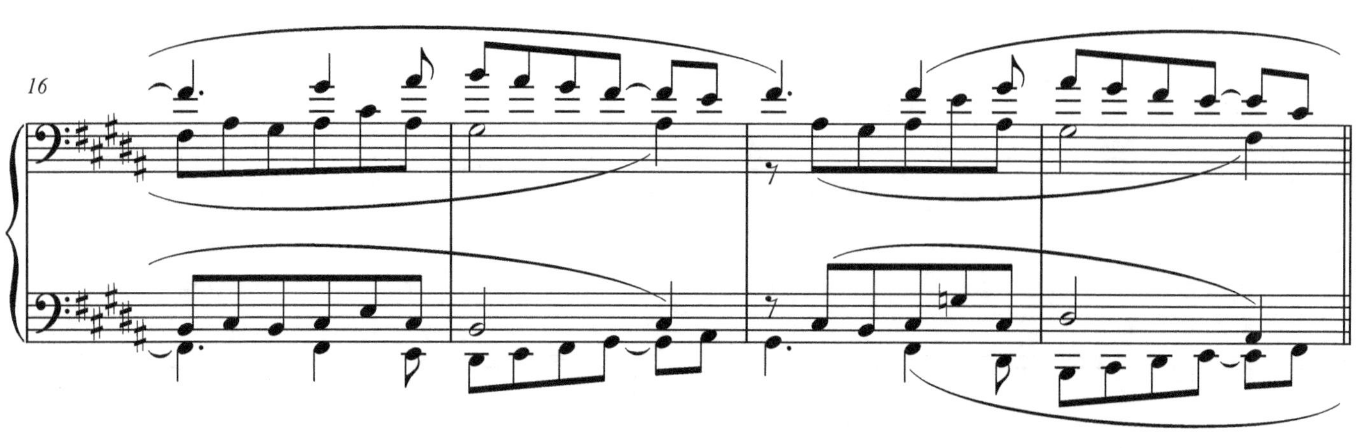

Piccadilly Circus

for Jovanni-Rey Verceles de Pedro

Jeremy Siskind

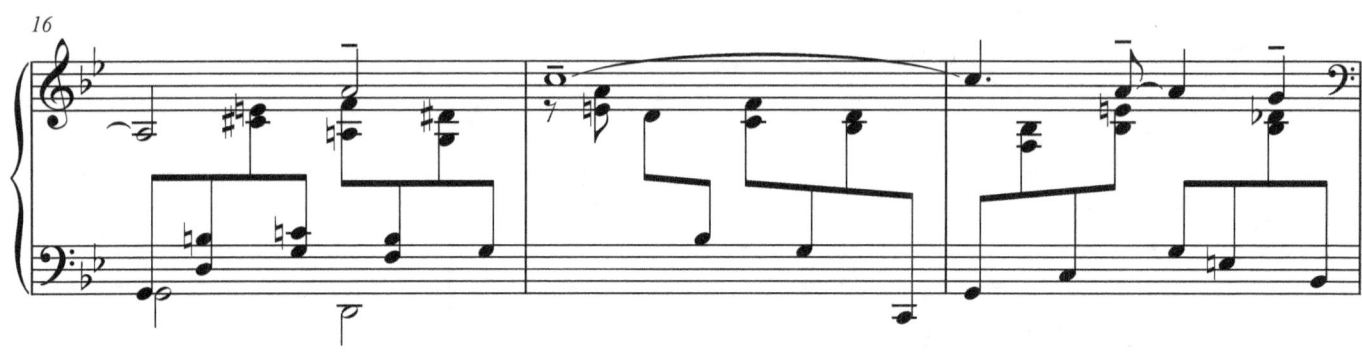

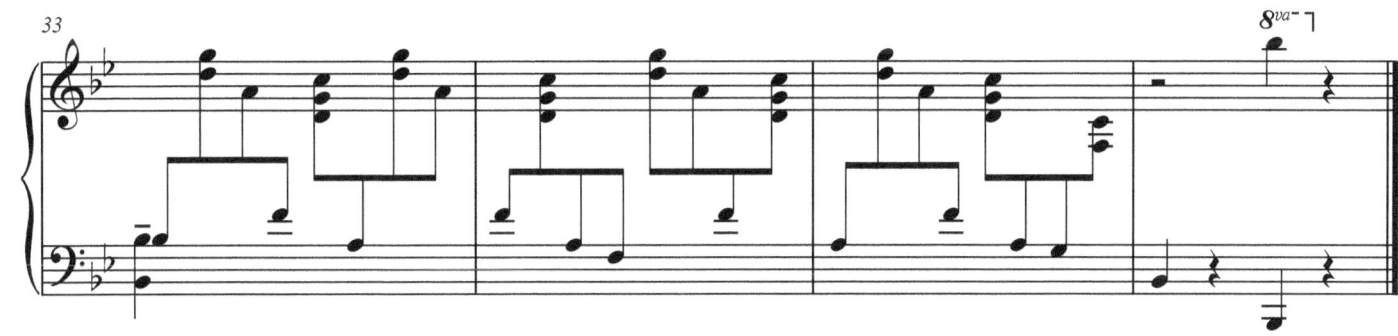

Piccadilly Circus
Optional Improvisation Instructions

Use this shorter ending to lead into the improvisation. Let a couple beats go by, then start the improvisation at a new tempo, a bit faster than the etude, and in swing feel. You can play a 4-measure jazz "solo fill" line to lead into the new feel and tempo.

Before Improvisation

a sample 4-measure "solo fill"

Improvise over the following 32-measure form, starting with a two-feel and evolving with the music.

Begin Improvisation

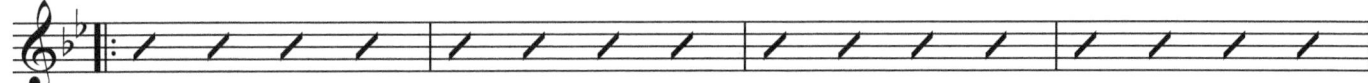

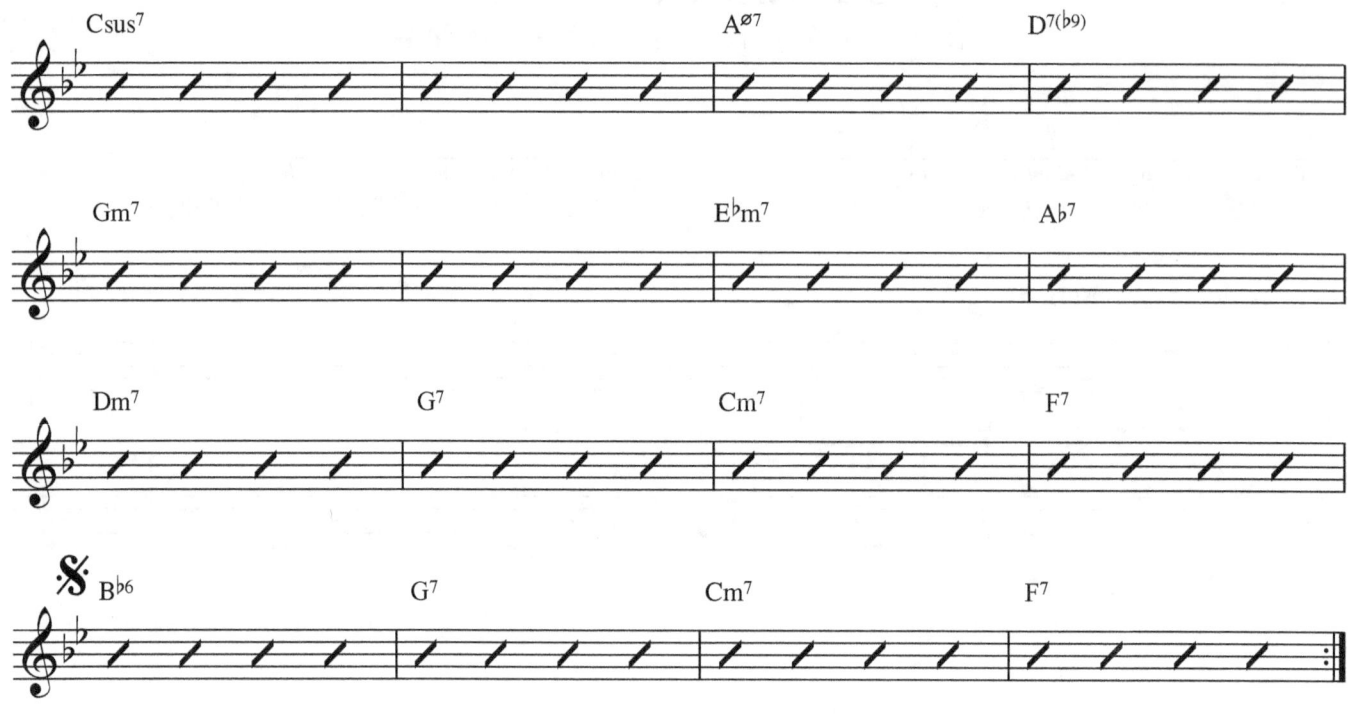

On the last time at the "sign," find some way to wrap up the solo. Then, set up the first melody note (F) in measure 1. Take as much time as you like to transition between these sections.

Here's one posisble "wrap up"

Here's one possible "set up"

Play the entire piece once more, but bridge the sections by easing into the tempo with extreme pushing and pulling, rather than starting suddenly in tempo. Generally, measure 17 is a good place to arrive in tempo.

After Improvisation

Temple Bells

Jeremy Siskind

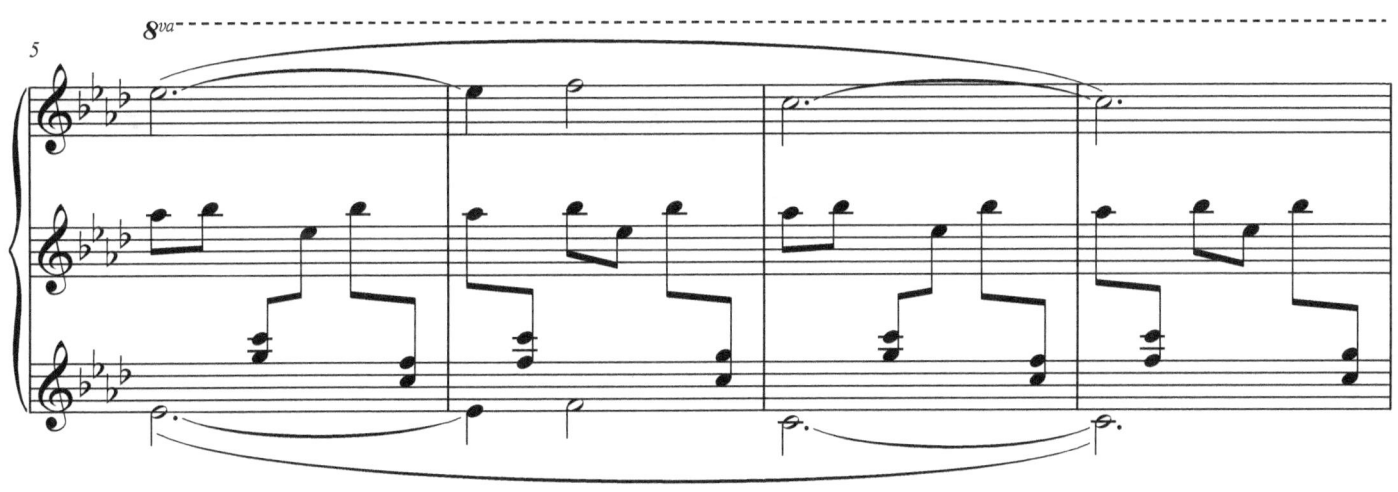
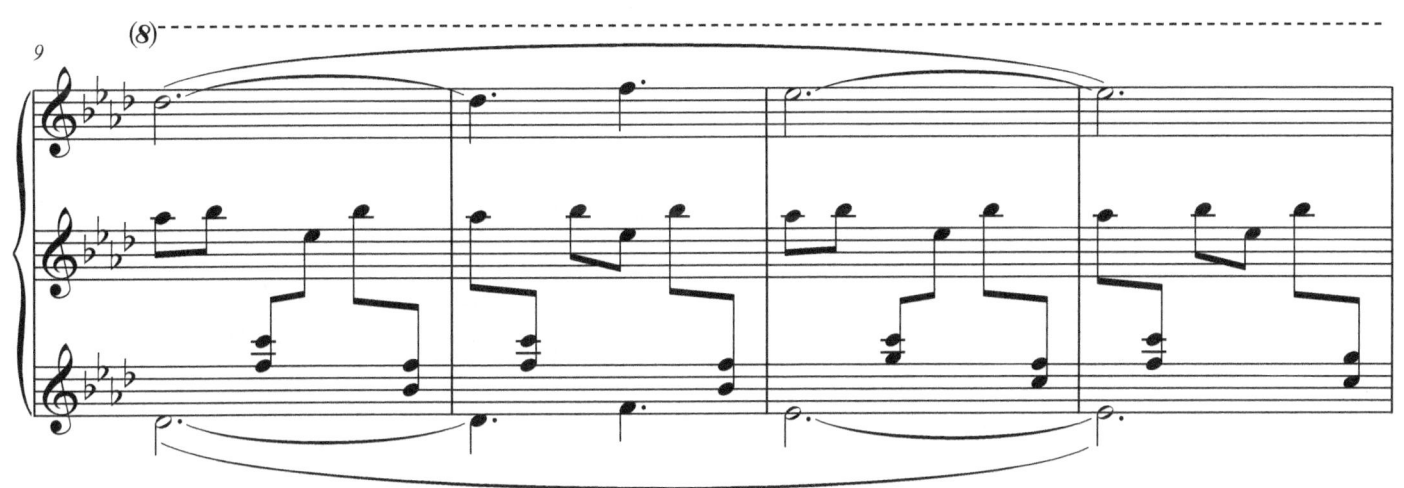

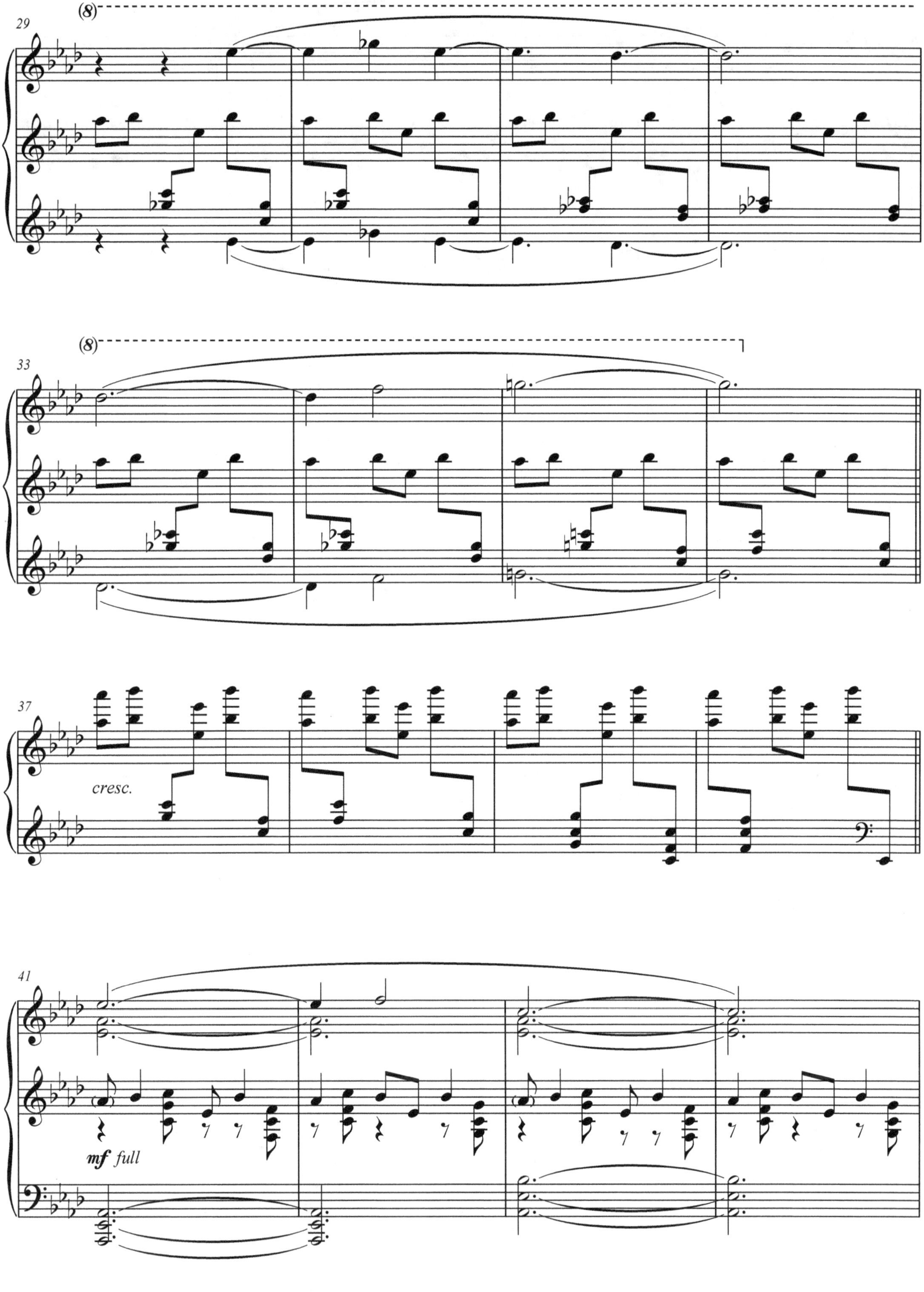
(8)
29
(8)
33
37
cresc.
41
mf full

Temple Bells
Optional Improvisation Instructions

Use this alternate ending for the piece, starting at measure 65, to lead into the improvisation section.

Before Improvisation

Start playing the ostinato below alone with the chords. Then, phase out the ostinato in favor of free right-hand improvisation. It can be nice to refer back to the ostinato periodically.

Begin Improvisation

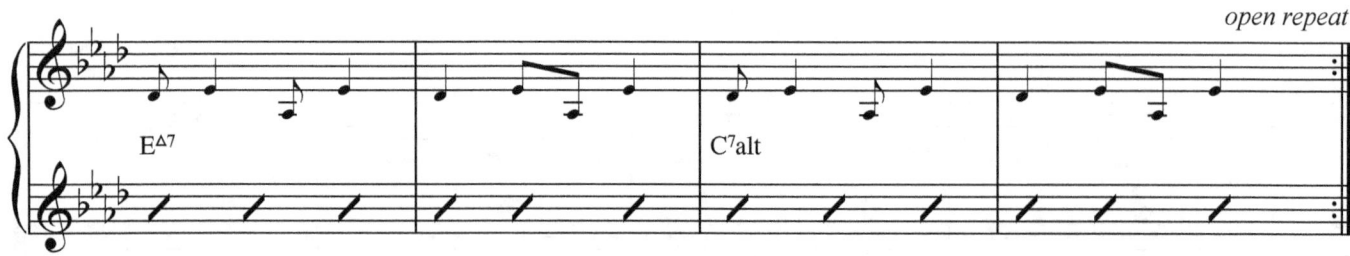

40

As the improvisation ends, phase the ostinato back in and add the original ostinato above to serve as a bridge back into the through-composed version.

After Improvisation

original ostinato

ostinato for improv

For the final statement of the melody, play as follows. For reference, these measures correspond to measures 5-20.

Continue on. For reference, the following measures correspond with measures 57-end.

Floating

Jeremy Siskind

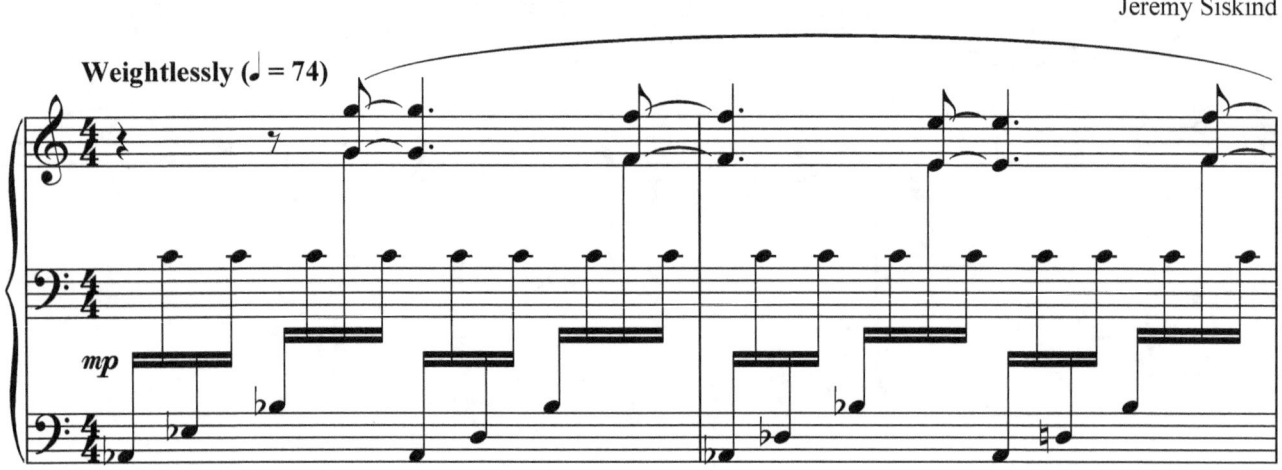
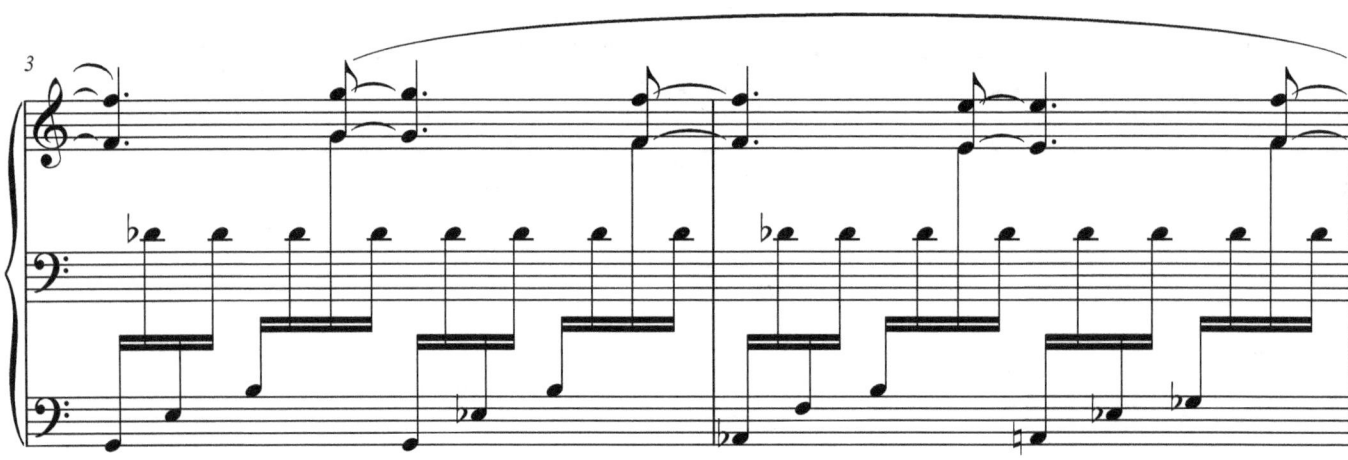
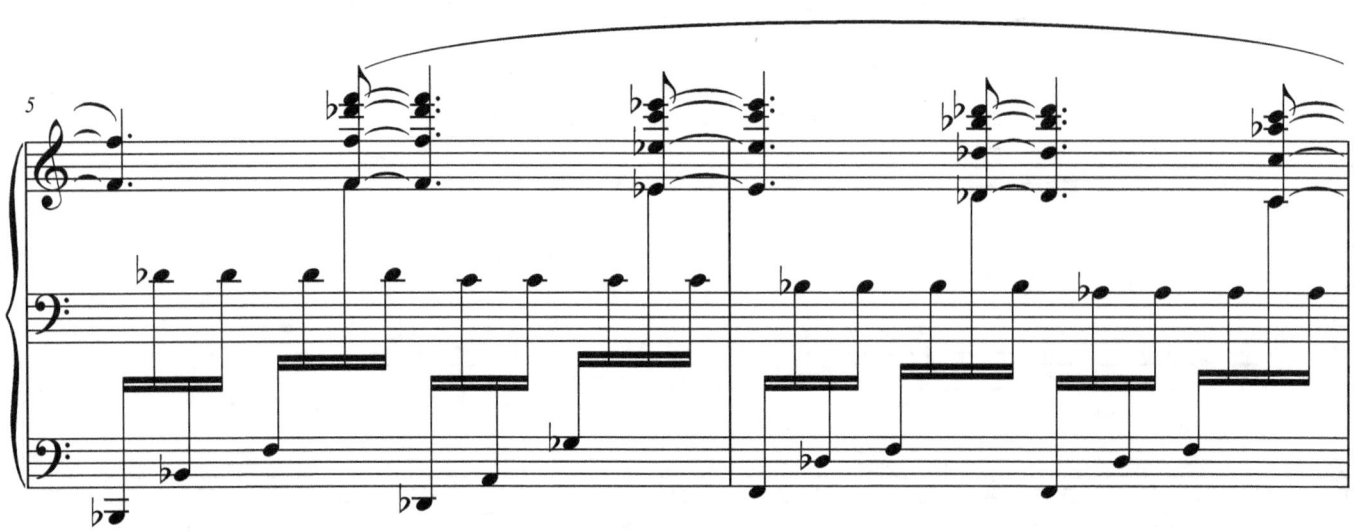

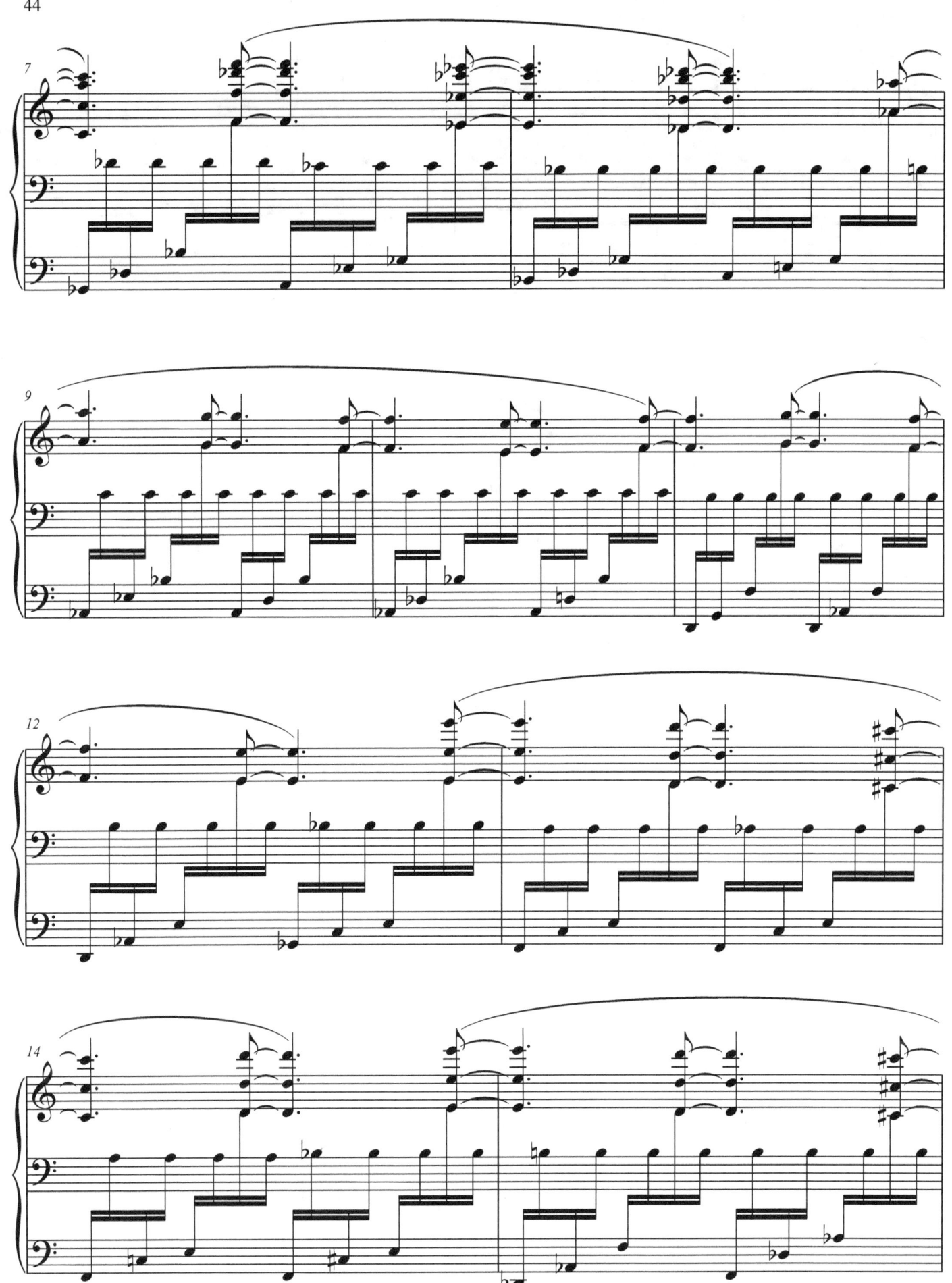

Floating
Optional Improvisation Instructions

The improvisation section for "Floating" begins after the "double bar" following measure 44.

Before Improvisation

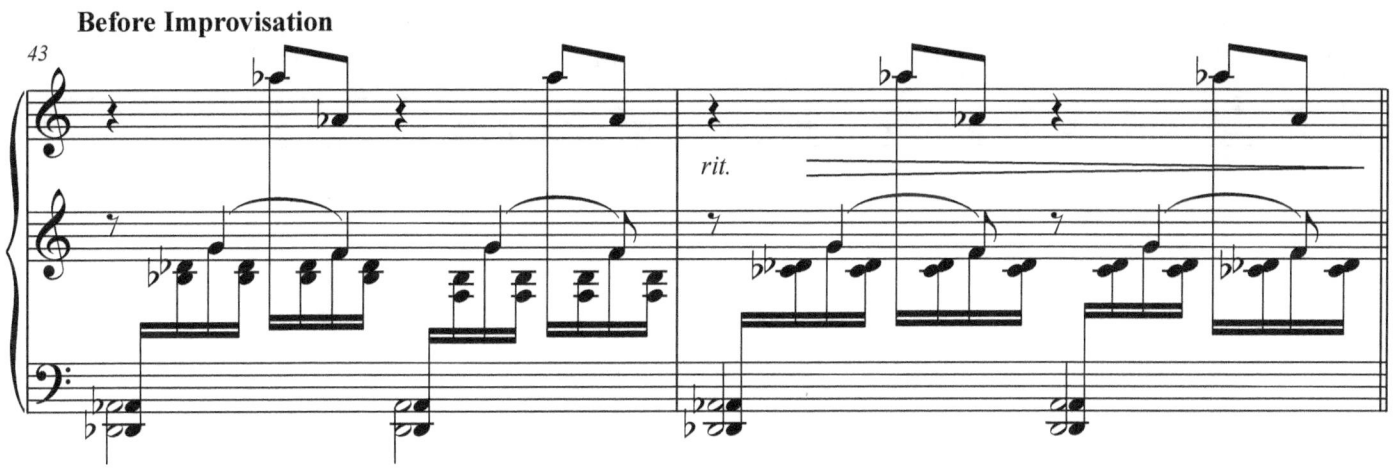

Create an improvisation on this chord progression while maintaining the feeling of the pulsing off-beat 16th notes. The feel could resemble a mid-tempo bossa nova. Repeat as many times as you like and then go to the "last x only" ending, which resolves on a held C major chord.

Begin Improvisation

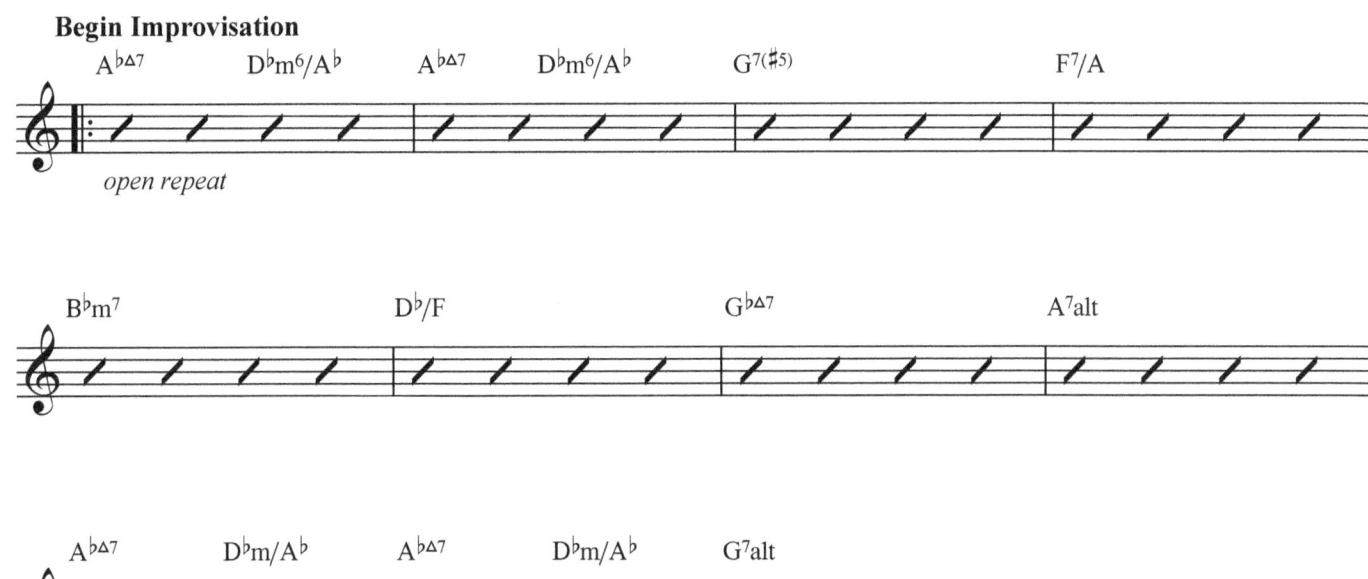

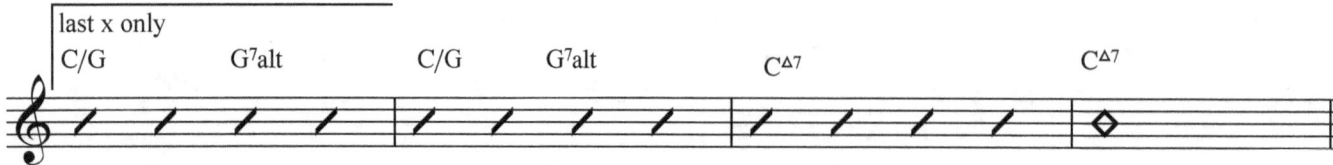

After improvising, play a shortened recapitulation as follows. For reference, the measure numbers given here reflect the corresponding spots in the original piece.

After Improvisation

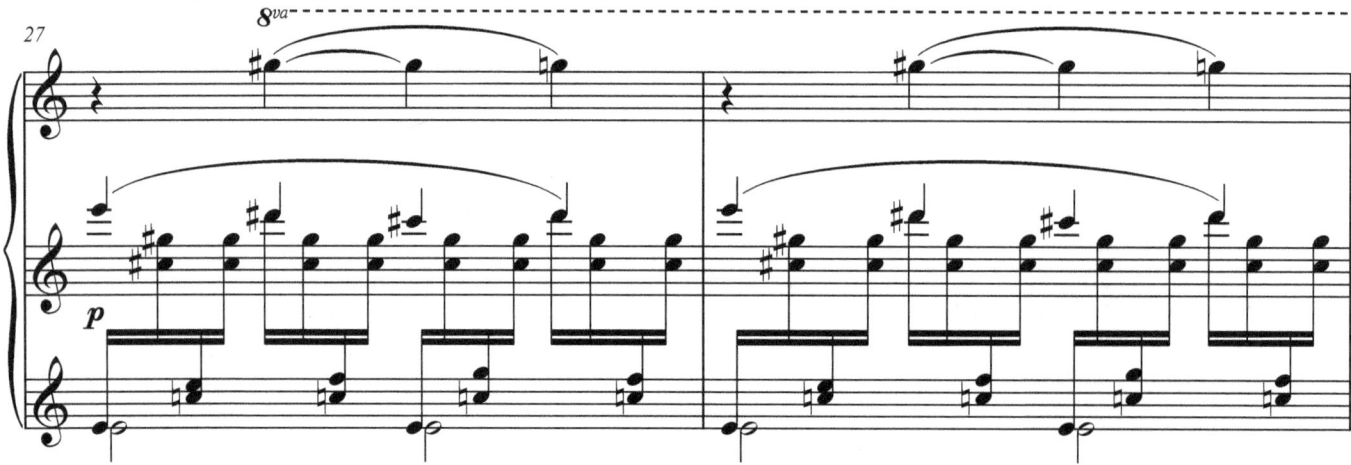

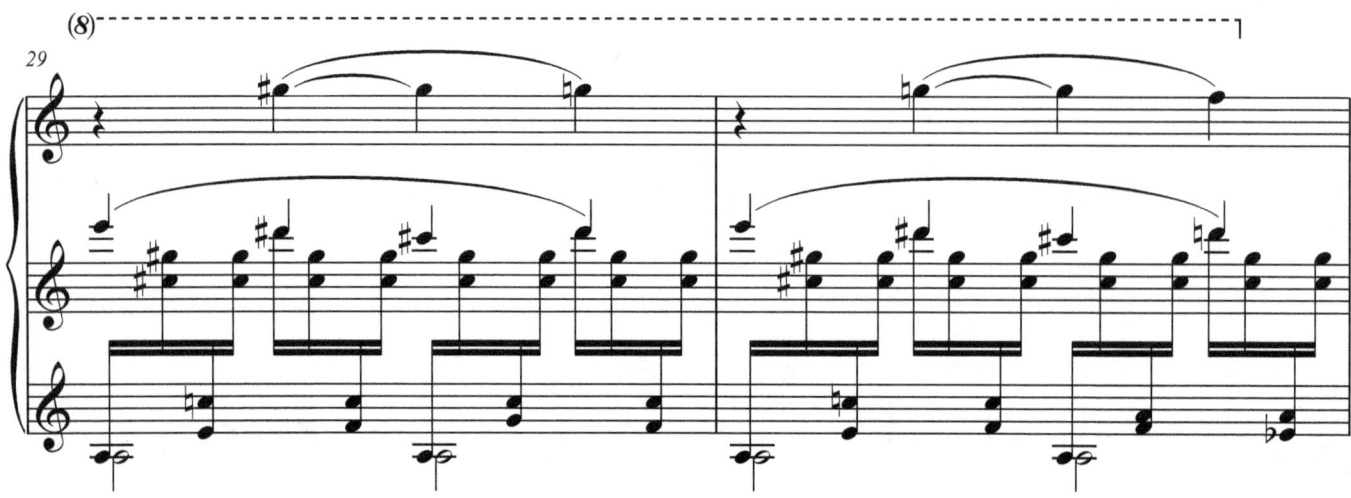

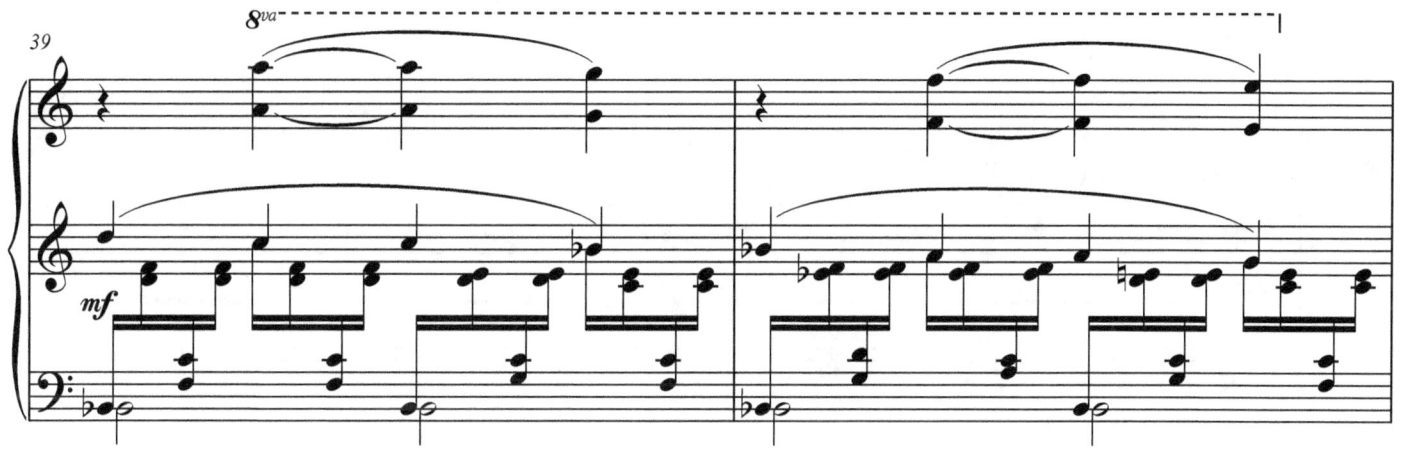

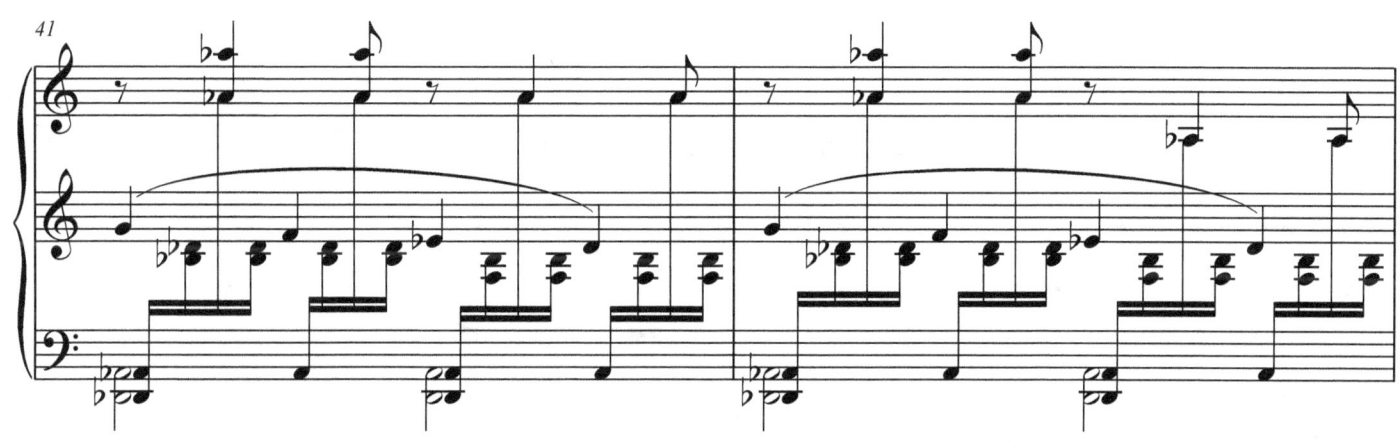

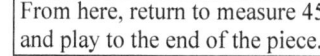

From here, return to measure 45 and play to the end of the piece.

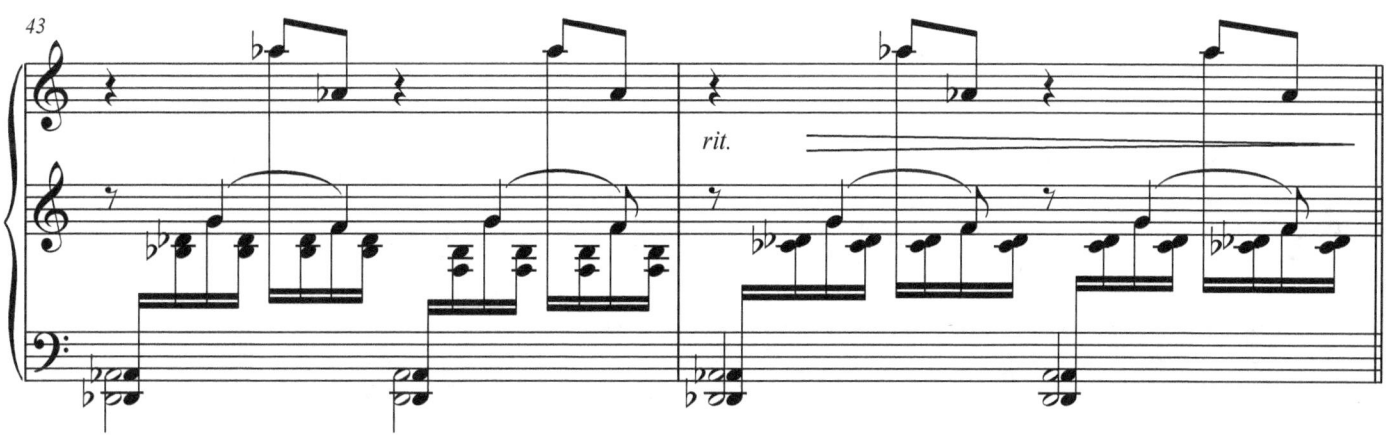

Blues

Jeremy Siskind

Aggressively (♪ = 310)

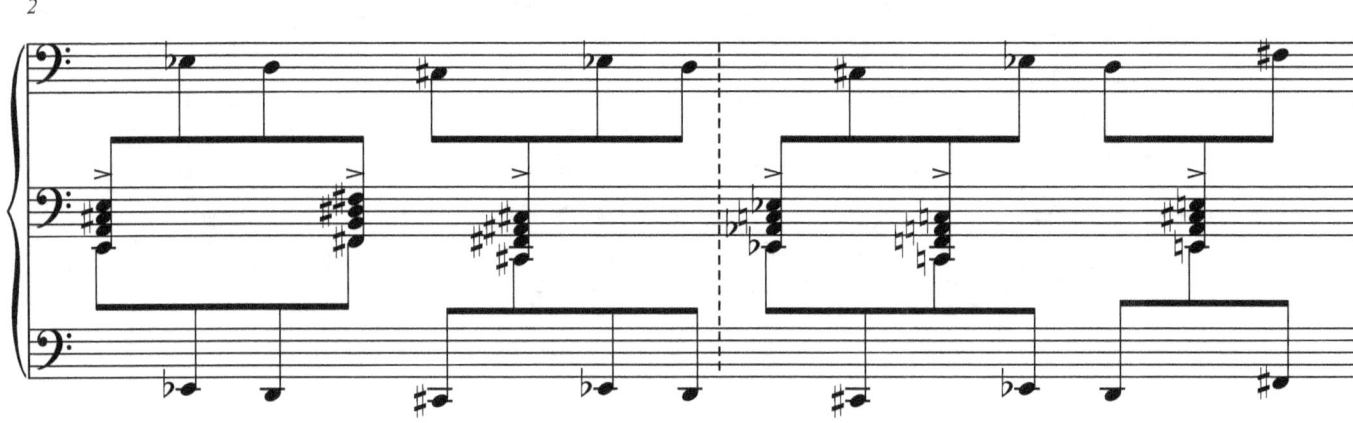

54

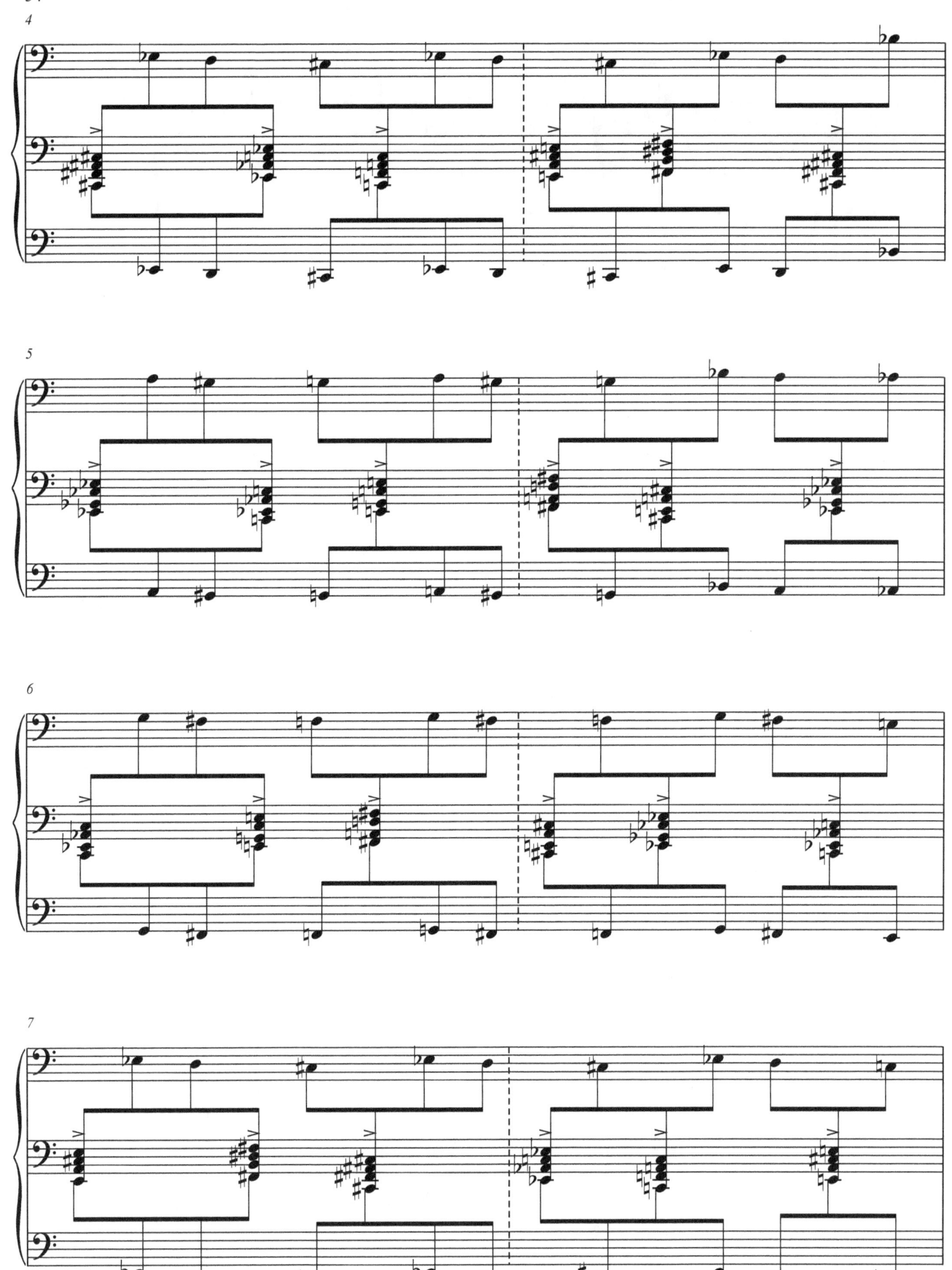

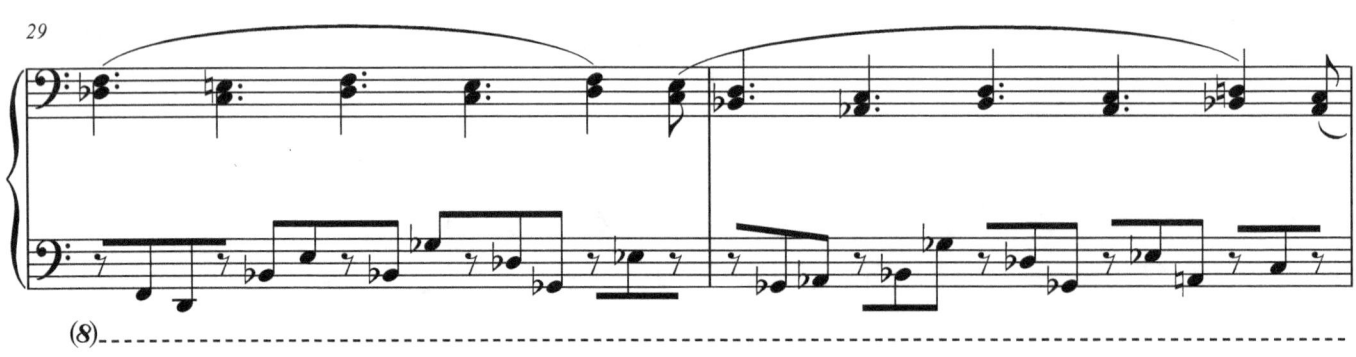
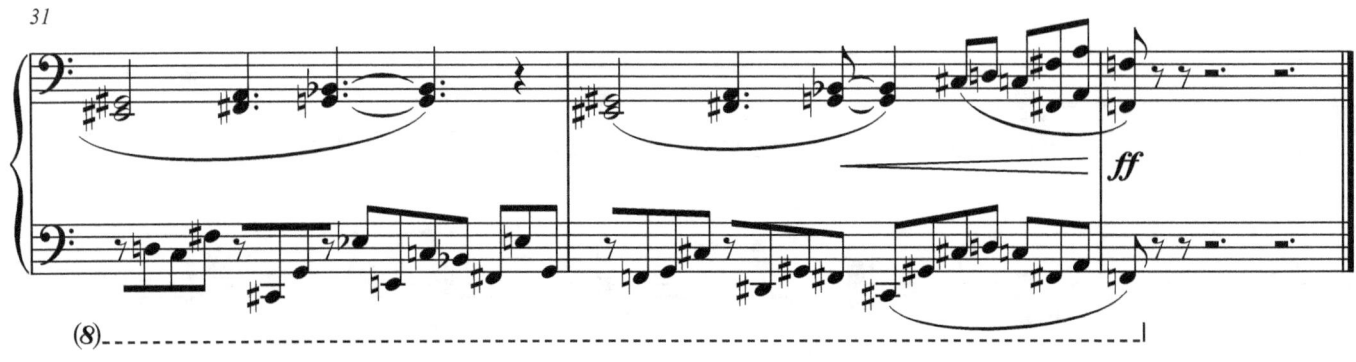

Blues
Optional Improvisation Instructions

To improvise on "Blues," play all the way to the end of the piece, but switch to 4/4 at measure 32 so that the "final" note (F) comes on the "and of 4."

Before Improvisation

Improvise over a loose, modal version of a "12-bar blues" progression in F. Feel free to add dissonant notes to match the character of the through-composed material.

To avoid having the piece sound like the "bottom dropped out," keep consistent 8th notes going in your left-hand. The left-hand can resemble boogie woogie style. I've written one possible example for the first 2 measures below.

Begin Improvisation

(one possible bassline)

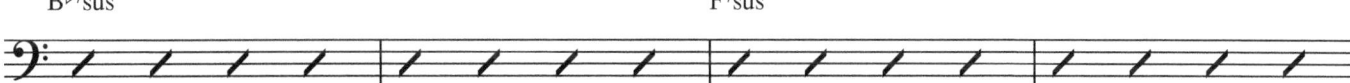

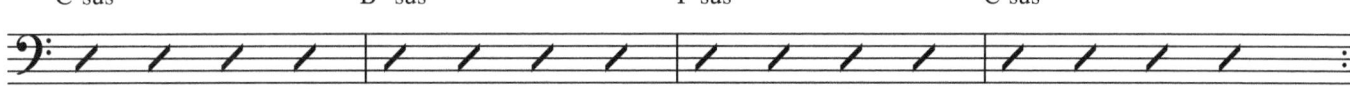

Wind down your improvisation to a medium dynamic so you can smoothly enter back in to the written material at measure 9.

After Improvisation

61

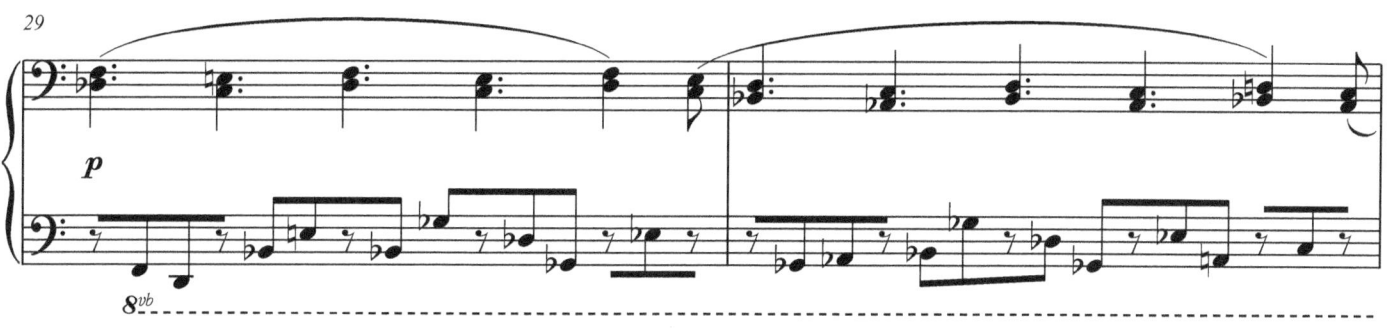

Continue on to the ending. For your reference, these measures correspond to measures 29-33 of the original score.

Enchanted Forest
for Eric and Sydney Fisher

Jeremy Siskind

Loosely, as though under a spell

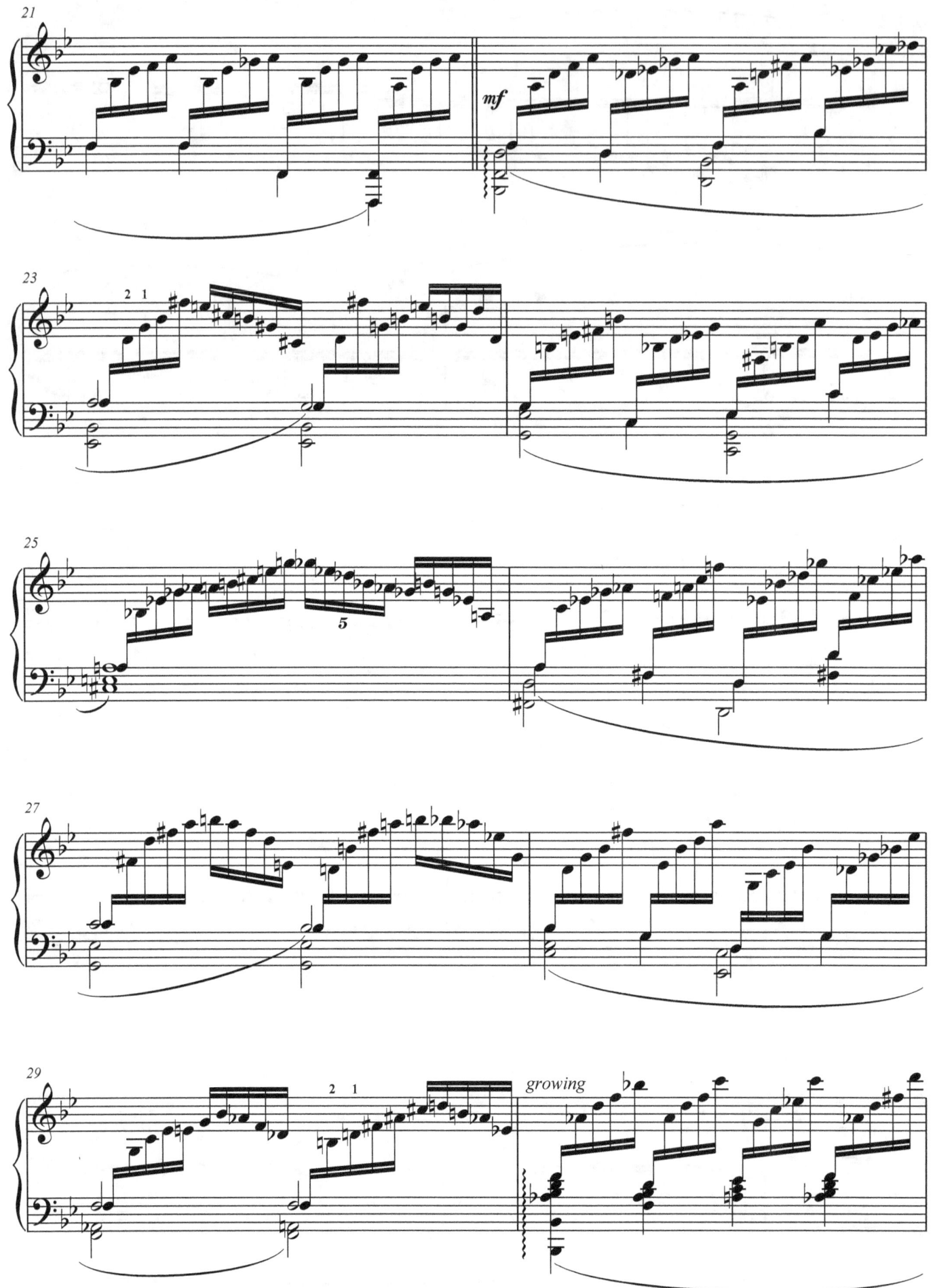

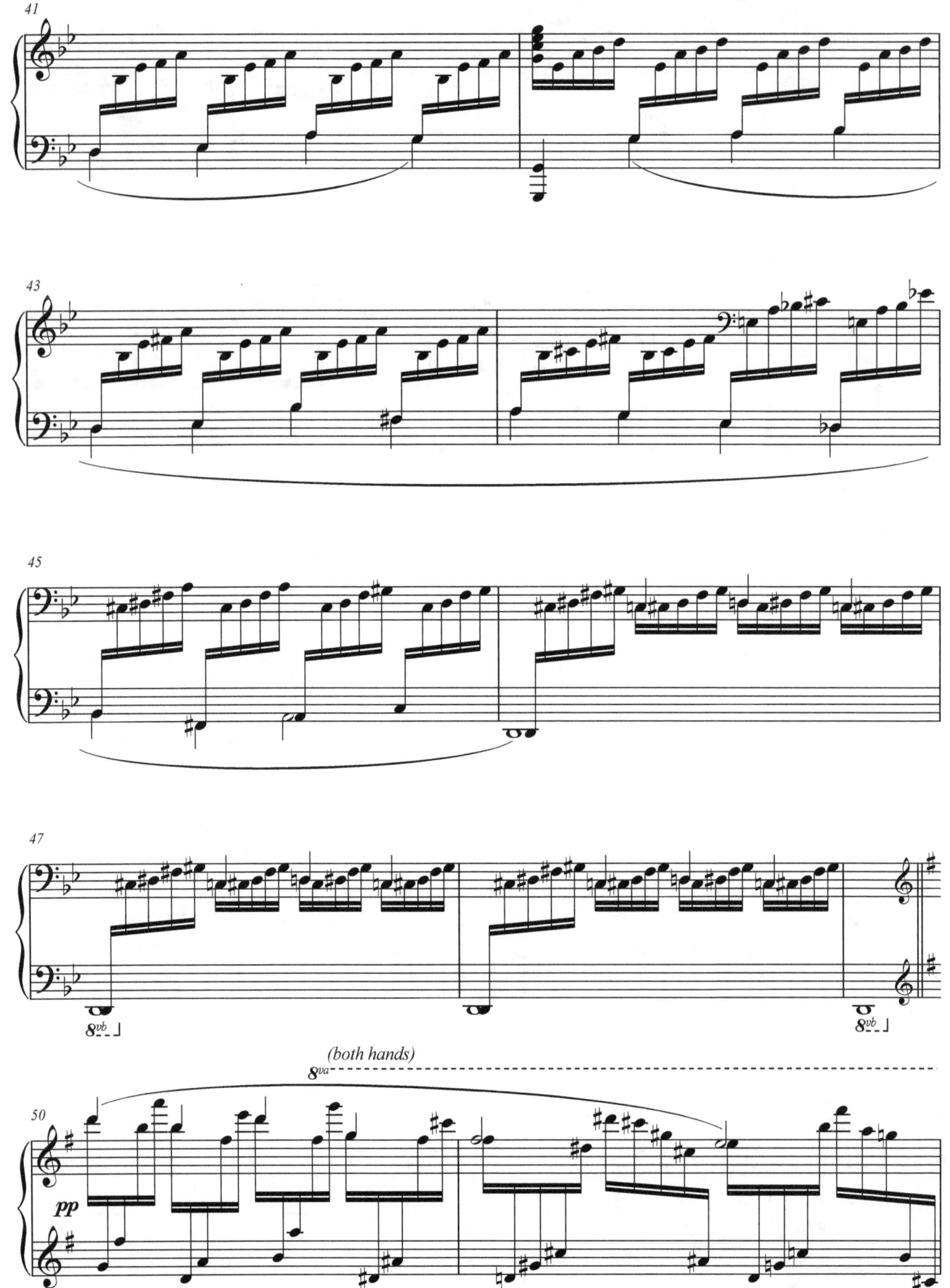

Enchanted Forest
Optional Improvisation Instructions

The improvisation section for "Enchanted Forest" is an open improvisation leading into the key change after measure 49. The improvisation can be nearly anything you'd like so long as it leads smoothly into G major.

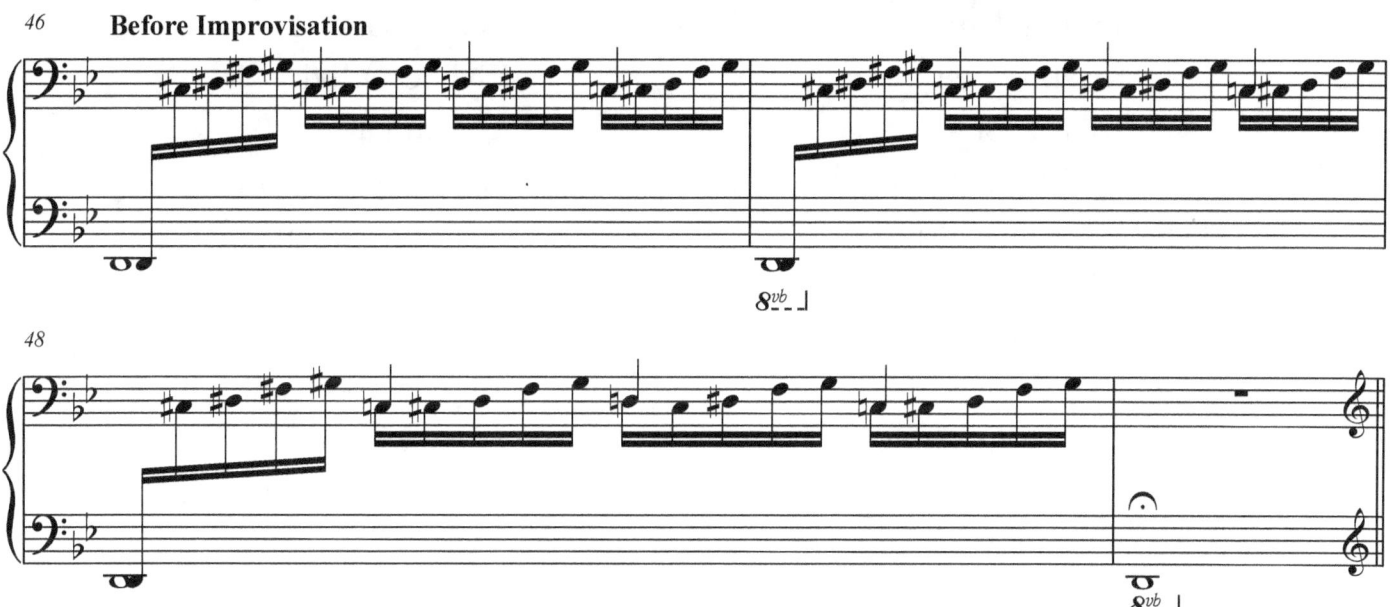

Begin improvisation Improvise freely, 1-3 minutes

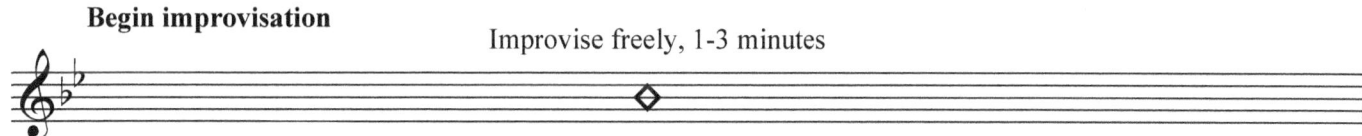

After the improvisation, continue to bar 50 and the end of the piece.

Special Thanks To

Ann DuHamel	Heidi Grimes
Kristina Lee	Sylvie Ollivier
Wai Leong	Sam Farley
Ellyn and Andrew Siskind	Mike and Julie Dana
Dr. Leonidas Lagrimas	Nancy Woo
Susan and Tom Brooks	Kaori Tanioka
Yoshimi	John Arida
Daniel R. Gustin	Doug Scarborough
Uncle Lloyd and Aunt Jo	Ellie Merriam
Bobby and Mary Gianfagna	Bill and Maggie Rousseau
Uncle Mark and Aunt Michele	Louise Wright
Rose Grace and Steven Halpern	Brian Gatchell
Fred Siskind	Katherine Lee
Ken and Esther Okajima	Debra Green Designs
Sydney and Eric Fisher	Sarah Siskind
Stella Ramirez	Robin Shoemaker
Paul Gilliland	Sue Onishenko
Shirley Knudson	Ryan A. Baca
Megan Chang	Richard and Mary Vallens
Frederic Chiu	Donna Dahm
Richard Messenger	Sean Kawanami
Steve and Connie Lyman	David and Satomi Pellerin
Cindy Ovokaitys	Bill Maxey
Dave Meder	Bob Avzaradel
Su-Shing Chiu	Matt Valerio
Kathleen Theisen	Alex Hurvitz and Family
Jim and Fran Antenore	Kaya Baird
Percebe Music	Silvia Roederer
Ray McCurrie	Arkady and Ella Serebryannik
Emily J. Black	Robert Chasan
Felicia Ruffman	Matt and Mary Ellen Merriam
	Emily Black

www.ingramcontent.com/pod-product-compliance
Lightning Source LLC
Chambersburg PA
CBHW081156290426
44108CB00018B/2576